LOOKING AT THE ZULU

Photographs and Text by Roger and Pat de la Harpe

STRUIK

Sipho and Thandi sit around the fire in their grandmother's hut, listening to her tales about the Zulu people, about how, a long, long time ago Shaka, the king of the Zulus, conquered many other tribes and formed the powerful Zulu nation. It was he who had started the customs and traditions that their grandmother insists they learn about and practice. They listen with pride as they hear about the Zulu kingdom which stretches from the Drakensberg Mountains to the Indian Ocean on the eastern side of South Africa.

Later, when the fire is low and they are tired, Sipho goes to sleep in his mother's hut *(indlu)* and Thandi in her mother's. Though they are brother *(umfowethu)* and sister *(dadewethu)*, they have different mothers, for in the Zulu culture a man may have more than one wife. Sipho's mother is the first wife and this means that she is the most important one. Their father is a wealthy man and can afford three wives and each wife has her own hut. Like other Zulu villages *(imizi)*, all the huts are built in a circle around the cattle pen.

The next morning, Sipho herds the goats and Thandi helps her mother with the housework. They have chores to do every day and often there seems little time to play. Nevertheless, they try to make their work fun. The girls help with the cooking, looking after their younger brothers and sisters, and collecting firewood and water. The boys tend the cattle *(inkomo)* and goats and learn about warrior traditions and bush lore from the older men in the family.

Thandi stirs the maize porridge in the three-legged iron pot (right) which bubbles and hisses over the fire. The family will eat the porridge with curdled milk, pumpkin and wild spinach. They will not eat meat today as it is only eaten on special occasions. Her mother prepares a pot of sorghum beer for her husband who is busy making spears and shields (above). When the family gets together at meal times, the children learn about Zulu customs and manners from their parents.

Sipho wears very little as he hurries home in the summer heat. Men and boys traditionally wear strips of leather hanging from their waists, while young girls dress in short, beaded skirts and headbands (above). After they are married, the girls wear pleated leather skirts and large, round headdresses, which they make from wool and clay. Sipho and Thandi look forward to dressing up for their older sister's wedding in a few weeks' time. They will use beads, feathers and animal skins but only the chief (right) can wear leopard skin.

As he reaches home, Sipho sees his father in the cattle pen admiring his large herd of cows and bulls. Like all Zulu men, his father has a great love for his Nguni cattle and, aided by their different colours and patterns, he can remember each animal by name. Sipho knows that cattle are very important in their culture, that they are a sign of wealth and that one day he will need them to pay for his bride. If he has many cattle like his father, he will be able to afford more than one wife.

The 11 cows paid as bride price *(lobola)* for Sipho and Thandi's sister are now with the rest of the herd. She agreed to get married only after her boyfriend had spoken to her many times down at the river while she collected water. As is the custom, she had pretended not to like him and had ignored him. He was very surprised and happy when one day her sisters and friends brought him the string of white engagement beads she had made for him to wear around his neck.

The Zulus love to wear colourful beadwork and Thandi has already learnt how to make necklaces, headbands, belts and skirts in bright colours. Like other Zulu women, her mother weaves grass baskets and mats (right) for use in their home, as well as making clay pots for cooking and brewing beer. Woodcarving is traditionally done by the men and Sipho has been taught by his older brothers how to carve spoons, bowls, spears and sticks.

At last the wedding day dawns and people start to arrive from all over the area. Everyone is very excited and the guests look forward to beer drinking, feasting and dancing. First the bride (above) and her family (right) dance and sing and then it is the turn of the groom and his family. The dancers kick and stamp their feet and blow whistles amid clapping and singing. Soon it is time for what all the young men have been waiting for — the stick fighting. This is a great sport and Zulu boys learn the rules and different positions at an early age.

Sipho has his own fighting sticks, as well as a short stick with a big knob at the end for hunting, a straight, thin one for herding the goats and a very special long one for practising his spear throwing. He is still too young to use a proper spear but he will when he is older and more responsible. Sticks, spears and shields are very important to Zulu men and it would not be right for a man to be out walking without a stick. He carries a shield and stick to all their ceremonies but most especially to weddings.

Zulu people are superstitious and everyone respects the traditional healer *(inyanga)* and diviner *(sangoma)*, as they have special powers. The diviner (above) chases away evil spirits and the traditional healer (right) treats sick people with mixtures of tree bark, roots and herbs. Sipho and Thandi's uncle had been to see a diviner a little while ago as his crops would not grow and he thought someone had cast a spell on them. The diviner had given him medicine *(muthi)* to sprinkle on his lands to keep the bad spirits away.

A few Zulu words that Sipho and Thandi think you should know:

Hello	*Sawubona*
Thank you	*Yabonga*
Hut	*Indlu*
Village	*Umuzi*
Yes	*Yebo*
Diviner	*Sangoma*
Traditional healer	*Inyanga*
Medicine	*Muthi*
Brother	*Umfowethu*
Sister	*Dadewethu*
Cattle	*Inkomo*
Bride price	*Lobola*

Acknowledgements

The authors would like to thank the staff at Shakaland and at Simunye Zulu Lodge near Eshowe, for their assistance.

Struik Publishers (Pty) Ltd
(a member of The Struik Publishing Group (Pty) Ltd)
Cornelis Struik House
80 McKenzie Street
Cape Town 8001

Reg. No.: 54/00965/07

First published in 1998

Copyright © 1998 in published edition:
Struik Publishers (Pty) Ltd
Copyright © 1998 in text:
Pat and Roger de la Harpe
Copyright © 1998 in photographs:
SIL/Pat and Roger de la Harpe with the exception of those on pages 4 – SIL/W. Kirr, 7 – SIL/S. Adey and 22 – SIL/L. Hoffman.
SIL = Struik Image Library

Editor: Glynne Newlands
Concept design: Laurence Lemmon-Warde
Designer: Dominic Robson
Cover design: Dominic Robson

Reproduction: Unifoto (Pty) Ltd
Printing and binding:
National Book Printers, Drukkery Street, Goodwood, Western Cape

All rights reserved. No part of this publication may be reproduced, stored in a retrieval system or transmitted in any form or by any means, electronic, mechanical, photocopying, recording or otherwise, without the prior written permission of the copyright owner(s).

ISBN 1 86872 126 4